100% UNOFFICIAL

BILLIE EILISH

A MUST-HAVE GUIDE TO THE MOST TALKED ABOUT TEEN ON THE PLANET

First published in Great Britain in 2020 by Dean,
an imprint of Egmont UK Limited,
2 Minster Court, 10th floor, London EC3R 7BB
www.egmont.co.uk

Written by Amy Wills
Designed by Martin Aggett

This book is an original creation by Egmont UK Limited

100% Unofficial: Billie Eilish copyright © Egmont UK Limited 2020

ISBN 978 1 4052 9899 5
71150/001
Printed in Italy

All rights reserved. No part of this publication may be reproduced, stored in a retrieval system, or transmitted, in any form or by any means, electronic, mechanical, photocopying, recording or otherwise, without the prior permission of the publisher and copyright owner.

This book is 100% independent and unofficial and is not endorsed by and has no connection with the people or persons featured, or with any organisation or individual connected in any way whatsoever with the people or persons featured. Every care has been taken in the researching and writing of this book.

Egmont takes its responsibility to the planet and its inhabitants very seriously. We aim to use papers from well-managed forests run by responsible suppliers.

BILLIE EILISH

A MUST-HAVE GUIDE TO THE MOST TALKED ABOUT TEEN ON THE PLANET

Amy Wills

100% UNOFFICIAL

Billie cleans up at the 2020 Grammys

ULTIMATE GUIDE TO BILLIE EILISH

CONTENTS

WHO IS BILLIE EILISH?	6
THE EARLY YEARS	8
A STAR IS BORN	10
6 REASONS WE LOVE BILLIE	12
BILLIE BY NUMBERS	14
SHE'S IN FASHION	16
BEAUTY SECRETS	18
6 FACTS ABOUT BILLIE	20
BILLIE'S BARNET	22
WHEN WE ALL FALL ASLEEP - WHERE DO WE GO?	24
THE WORLD ACCORDING TO BILLIE	26
BILLIE ON TOUR	28
BEST MUSIC VIDEOS	30
BILLIE VS FAME	32
WHO IS FINNEAS?	34
BILLIE'S FAVOURITE THINGS	36
THE ULTIMATE BILLIE PLAYLIST	38
BILLIE OPENS UP	40
VOICE OF A GENERATION	42
SCREEN IDOL	44
BILLIE'S INFLUENCES	46
BILLIE EXPLAINS IT ALL	48
TIMES BILLIE WAS ALL OF US	50
BILLIE VS SOCIAL MEDIA	52
FAMOUS FANS	54
BILLIE ON LOVE	56
THINGS BILLIE HATES	58
ALBUM NUMBER TWO	60
BILLIE LOVES HER FANS	62

100% UNOFFICIAL

WHO IS BILLIE EILISH?

How one teenage pop star is reinventing the music industry

In October 2016, 14-year-old Billie Eilish, uploaded her first song, '**Ocean Eyes**', to **SoundCloud** late one night in her LA bedroom. She had only intended for one person to listen to it: her dance teacher. When she woke up the next day, the song had **gone viral** around the world with over 1,000 listens (it's now had around **34.6million**).

Her music defies genre – it's been called pop, EDM, industrial, trap and even jazz - her voice ranges from a muted whisper to a belted-out chorus, and her strange lyrics blend point of view and gender roles. **Speaking specifically to the anxieties of Gen Z** (her album addresses climate change, teen suicide and sobriety) and also dealing with timeless themes like love and death, Billie Eilish has fans of every age.

From her first song, things skyrocketed. Eilish (pronounced eye-lish) signed a record deal with Darkroom and Interscope Records. Her first single '**bad guy**' went straight to the top of the charts, making her the first artist born this century to have a US No1.

ULTIMATE GUIDE TO BILLIE EILISH

She released her first album, **When We All Fall Asleep, Where Do We Go?** in 2019 to universal critical acclaim and record-breaking chart domination.

With her own distinctive punk style, 'neo-goth' aesthetic and irreverent social media voice, she challenges expectations of what a female pop star can sound like, look like, and publicly say.

She's played **Coachella**, **Glastonbury** and performed at **The Oscars**. She's the youngest ever artist to record the **Bond theme** tune. At the **2020 Grammys**, Billie Eilish made history as the second artist in the show's history to win all four major categories: **Best New Artist, Record of the Year**, Album of the Year, and Song of the Year. At 18, she's the **youngest Grammy winner to win all four nominations** on the same night and the first woman to do so.

07

100% UNOFFICIAL

THE EARLY YEARS

Although it feels like she came out of nowhere and took over the world, Billie has a backstory …

Billie Eilish Pirate Baird O'Connell was born in **2001** in the **Highland Park** area of **Los Angeles**. This now popular place was not always so appealing. Billie describes it as being *"really sketchy"* during her *childhood*.

Billie was also home-schooled, and her mum taught her a beginner's songwriting course. "When I see movies set in summertime, that's what my life was like all the time, but it doesn't mean I didn't learn," said Billie. "My mom would cook and she'd be like, 'How much goes into this?' And that's how we learned."

She lived with her *"built-in best friend"* and older brother **Finneas** (more on him later) and her parents **Maggie Baird** and **Patrick O'Connell**, who were jobbing actors. They were raised vegetarian and slept in a four-person family bed until Finneas was 10.

ULTIMATE GUIDE TO BILLIE EILISH

Little Billie loved dancing, horse riding and singing in the Los Angeles Children's Chorus. She was also a budding fashion designer, building costumes and making accessories from scratch.

Her dream was to be a dancer, until injuries meant she had to give it up. But dancing's loss was music's gain. *"I've always known that singing, writing music and performing is what I've wanted to do,"* she says. We are glad it worked out, Billie!

09

100% UNOFFICIAL

A STAR IS BORN

From making music in her bedroom to making history

'**Ocean Eyes**' was just the beginning. Although she was just 14, Billie signed a record deal with Intercope and, instead of just bringing out 'Ocean Eyes' as a single, she got to work on her EP. In the summer of 2017 she released '**Don't Smile At Me**'. "*My EP is called 'Don't Smile At Me' for a lot of reasons, but one of them would be when [someone tells you], 'Smile. Why aren't you smiling? It's so much more beautiful when you smile.'*"

Eilish finally dropped her long-awaited and first full-length album on March 29, 2019. Eilish was nervous just before **When We All Fall Asleep, Where Do We Go?** dropped, afraid people wouldn't love it like she did. "*I didn't want the world to be able to tell me how they feel about this thing I love,*" she confessed. "*But the response has been crazy.*" It went straight to the **top of the chart** in the **UK** and the **US**.

ULTIMATE GUIDE TO BILLIE EILISH

Two weeks later she began her album tour with a coveted slot at the music festival **Coachella**. She went on to win a clutch of awards, break records, be named **Billboard**'s woman of the year and record the song for the **James Bond** movie **No Time To Die**. And she's still only 18. **Wow!**

100% UNOFFICIAL

6 REASONS WE LOVE BILLIE

Err, 'cause she's the best ...

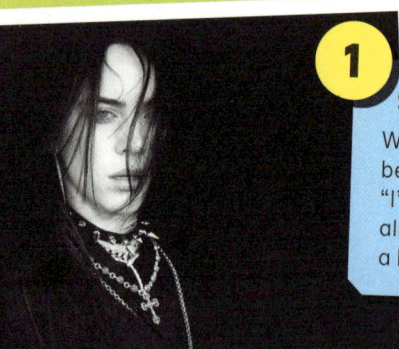

1

SHE KEEPS IT REAL

We can't think of many pop stars who would begin their debut album with the words "I've taken out my Invisalign and this is my album" but that's how Billie's kicks off. What a legend.

2

SHE'S POLITICAL

Billie has used her platform to speak out about everything from gun control to climate change. She recently took part in a campaign encouraging people to register to vote. Billie for President!

3

SHE'S A TRUE ORIGINAL

Billie has no interest in blending into the crowd. "I've always known what I want and who I wanted to be, what I wanted to wear and who I wanted to be seen as." You do you, Billie.

ULTIMATE GUIDE TO BILLIE EILISH

4

SHE CALLS OUT INJUSTICE

When Nylon magazine mocked up a strange cover of a naked, hair-less Billie, she wasn't going to take it lying down. She called them out as having done it without her consent in a totally justified response to a very uncool use of her image.

5

SHE JUST DOESN'T CARE

Whether she's wearing a head-to-toe baggy jumpsuit or dyeing her hair bright green, Billie has bad-ass confidence. "*I like to dress memorable,*" she says. "*I love being in people's heads, so if you are thinking about me, but what you're thinking about is like 'Oh, she looks so bad' or 'That's so ugly', I don't even care!*" We will remember this next time someone gives us *the look*.

6

SHE'S MADE POP COOL AGAIN

With so much talk about the music industry dying, Billie has resurrected it. She's made it cool to like pop. Billie, we salute you!

100% UNOFFICIAL

BILLIE BY NUMBERS

What's the secret to Billie's success? Let's figure it out

2.36 BILLION
The number of streams *When We All Fall Asleep, Where Do We Go?* had in 2019

5
The number of Grammy awards Billie has

59 MILLION
The number of followers Billie has on Instagram

£6 MILLION
Her estimated worth

28 MILLION
The number of Billie's subscribers on YouTube

12
The age she was when she fell for her 'first love' Justin Bieber

ULTIMATE GUIDE TO BILLIE EILISH

816 MILLION
Views for 'Bad Guy', her most-watched video on YouTube

800
Billie jokes her clothes are this many sizes to big for her

10,000
Hours is written on Finneas' wall to remind him of how much dedication is needed

13
The number of different hair colours Billie's had

13
The age she was when she recorded the vocals for 'Ocean Eyes'

5' 3"
How tall Billie is

2014
The year Billie went vegan

007
Billie is the youngest artist to record a Bond theme tune

8
The track on her album where she plays ukulele (it was originally called 7)

15

100% UNOFFICIAL

SHE'S IN FASHION

Billie's wardrobe is as distinctive as her music

From highlighter hair to oversized clothes, face masks to high-vis vests, Billie's fashion sense is like no one else's. *"I always wanted to wear whatever I wanted to wear. No one has ever told me otherwise even when I was a kid. Clothing is my safety net, it's like my security guard."*

FEBRUARY 2019
It's road safety, but make it fashion

SEPTEMBER 2018
Oversized, neon colours, totally rad – this look is 100% Billie

In May 2019, in an advert for **Calvin Klein**, Eilish shared with the world the reason she always wears baggy clothing. *"I never want the world to know everything about me,"* she says. *"That's why I wear big, baggy clothes. Nobody can have an opinion because they haven't seen what's underneath."*

ULTIMATE GUIDE TO BILLIE EILISH

She's also calling out the sexism in the music industry. *"If I was a guy and I was wearing these baggy clothes, nobody would bat an eye. There's people out there saying, 'Dress like a girl for once! Wear tight clothes you'd be much prettier and your career would be so much better!' No it wouldn't."* Girl power.

NOVEMBER 2019
Rocking head-to-toe Burberry and a full-face veil

NOVEMBER 2019
Who knew satin Gucci pyjamas, sneakers and two-tone green hair could look so good?

Cementing her status as a fashion icon, Billie recently designed fashion collections with **Urban Outfitters**, **Bershka**, and **H&M**. *"I really like fashion, I'm already doing a lot with it because it is just part of who I am. I feel like I might be a designer or stylist."* Watch this space.

17

100% UNOFFICIAL

BEAUTY SECRETS

We've collected all Billie's best tips so you don't have to rummage through her make-up bag!

Brow Power

Billie is known for her trademark full bushy eyebrows. Her make-up artist Robert Rumsey uses a brow pencil, to "draw the hairs in the direction of the natural growth. It's more modern than filling in the entire brow". Then he adds a clear brow gel to set the look.

The Billie basics

"Don't touch your face! I always make it a habit not to. I wash my face every night and apply a moisturiser or else my skin will flake off into a million pieces. Essentially, I always make sure to drink a lot of water, sleep and not touch my face."

ULTIMATE GUIDE TO BILLIE EILISH

Less is more

When it comes to her skin, Billie likes to keep it natural. "You don't need a ton of products," says Robert. "A good foundation and concealer. I prefer buildable products. I like translucent loose powder for the T-zone and cream highlighters that aren't sticky."

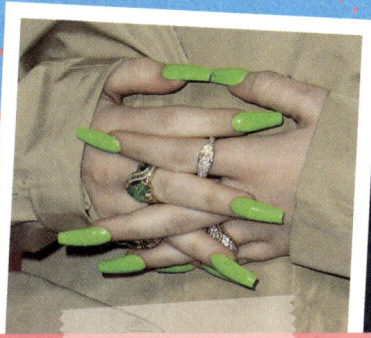

Got it nailed

Billie has started wearing long acrylic green nails, even wearing customised Gucci ones to the Grammys. But she often shares pictures on Instagram of broken nails.

Get rid of the gloss

Robert says he avoids two products when Billie performs on stage - lip gloss and sticky highlighter. "Billie has long hair and I don't want it sticking to her face," he told Yahoo.

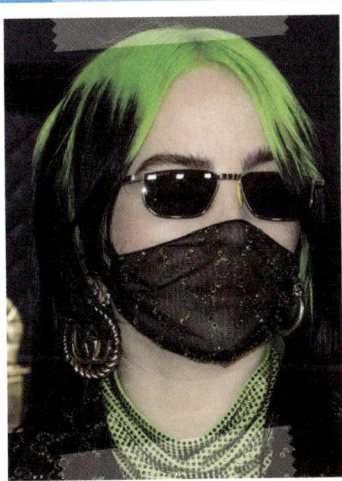

Go for glow

"My inspo for the AMAs was glow, glow, GLOW," said Robert. "I knew she was performing with fire around her. I kept the skin clean with flawless, bushy brows, and perfectly separated lashes. Always a wet lip."

And if all else fails ...

Wear a mask and sunnies. Duh.

19

100% UNOFFICIAL

6 FACTS ABOUT BILLIE

A few things you might not know about being Billie

ULTIMATE GUIDE TO BILLIE EILISH

1. SHE HAS SYNAESTHESIA
Billie has synesthesia, a condition in which senses seem to blend together because of neurosensory wire-crossing. It means objects such as words or numbers can be joined with a sensory perception such as smell, flavour or colour. According to Eilish, her song *'bad guy'* is red, yellow and the number seven.

2. SHE IS LACTOSE-INTOLERANT
Eilish grew up vegetarian and officially switched to a vegan lifestyle in 2014. Regarding her choice, she went to Tumblr to explain why she decided to go free of animal products in her diet. In 2018, she wrote on her blog, "*I went vegan like four years ago. there were a lot of reasons. I love animals and also I'm lactose intolerant.*"

3. SHE LOVES HORSES
Billie worked in barns to afford riding lessons. She recently collaborated with Urban Outfitters to donate money to Red Bucket Equine Rescue, an organisation that rehabilitates and rescues horses.

4. SHE'S A HORROR MOVIE FAN
Her favourite movie is *The Babadook*.

5. SHE HAS TOURETTE'S
In 2018, the singer confirmed that she had Tourette Syndrome, a condition which causes a person to have involuntary tics. She specifically experiences physical tics as opposed to verbal ones. "*I've taught myself ways of suppressing my tics and certain techniques to help reduce them when I don't want to be distracting in certain situations,*" she explained in an Instagram story.

6. SHE'S A MOVIE STAR (KIND OF)
As a child she recorded the background dialogue for films such as Diary of a Wimpy Kid, Ramona and Beezus, and the X-Men series.

100% UNOFFICIAL

BILLIE'S BARNET

Blue? Green? Black? Silver? Billie has had some serious transformations in the hair department

Her natural colour is light brown, but around 2017 she dyed it platinum white. She then went for a smoky grey colour. Normally associated with Grannies, on Billie it looked more Grammys.

Next she went bright green, and then bright blue. *"Here's what's annoying: I hate the color blue – it's my least favourite colour. I don't know how I ended up dying it blue."*

ULTIMATE GUIDE TO BILLIE EILISH

Then it was time to go black, or black with blue streaks, or black with neon green roots. Although it recently looked like she'd cut a mullet, this was an accidental thing – it got burnt while being dyed.

In her video for **'Xanny'**, Billie donned a brunette wig. She looks so … different?!

100% UNOFFICIAL

WHEN WE ALL FALL ASLEEP, WHERE DO WE GO?

A complete track by track breakdown

THE BEGINNING

The album's opening track, **'!!!!!!!'**, is just Billie slurping saliva, announcing "*this is the album,*" and descending into laughter. Then it's straight into pop-trap song **'bad guy'**, which uses a bass, a kick drum and finger clicks. Then there's **'Xanny'**. While recording this song, Billie and her brother created a sound inspired by a girl blowing cigarette smoke in someone's face alongside a drum kit and a jazz-inspired loop. So now we know what that sounds like.

THE MIDDLE

'You Should See Me in a Crown' is all blaring synths and electropop. Then **'All Good Girls Go To Hell'** is a punchy piano number. **'Wish You Were Gay'** is a jazzy pop song, and **'When the Party's Over'** was written after Finneas had left his date's house for "*kind of no reason*". We've all been there.

24

ULTIMATE GUIDE TO BILLIE EILISH

THE COVER

The shoot for the cover art took place on Billie's 17th birthday at a studio in LA and lasted 12 hours. Billie had prepared sketches for the album cover inspired by night terrors and lucid dreaming, and horror movies such as **The Babadook**. Photographer Kenneth Cappello added no additional lighting to the end photo so as to give the impression that "*a door was opening and that was the light coming into the bedroom.*" Eilish wore contact lenses to fill in her eyes completely with white.

MORE MIDDLE

'8' – appropriately-enough the eighth track on the album – is a ukulele-based lullaby. So it's quite a shift to **'My Strange Addiction'** a bass-heavy pop banger which samples 'The Office'. **'Bury A Friend'** is a minimalist electronica with synth melodies. The beat leads seamlessly into **'Ilomilo'** named after the videogame.

THE END

The final three tracks each talk about saying farewell, collectively reading '**Listen Before I Go**', '**I Love You**' and '**Goodbye**'. 'Goodbye', features a line of each of the album's tracks (with the exception of '!!!!!!!') in its lyrics in reverse order compared with how they appear in the album, beginning with a line from 'I Love You' and ending with a line from 'bad guy,' with clips from these songs layered quietly in reverse.

25

ULTIMATE GUIDE TO BILLIE EILISH

THE WORLD ACCORDING TO BILLIE

Say it, girl

"In the public eye, girls and women with strong perspectives are hated. If you're a girl with an opinion, people just hate you. That's so lame."

We are printing this out and sticking it on our bedroom wall.

"I've always done whatever I want and always been exactly who I am."

"There are always going to be bad things. But you can write it down and make a song out of it."

"I'm not going to say I'm cool. I just don't care at all, and I guess that's what people think is cool."

Aww.

"I feel like I write so that people can think of it as theirs. If my song is exactly about your life right now, then it is."

27

100% UNOFFICIAL

BILLIE ON TOUR

Never made it to a Billie Eilish concert? This is almost as good as seeing her live

COACHELLA
This was a big moment for Billie, she was one of the most talked-about performers at the festival. The crowd went crazy, and knew all the words to her songs, even if Billie didn't. While singing **'All the Good Girls Go To Hell'**, Billie forgot the lyrics. To be fair, the album only came out a few weeks before.

When she plays the song *'Copycat'* it often starts a moshpit

She uses creepy props

When a fan threw underwear on stage and it hit her she said *"OK, that's the energy, I get it"*

ULTIMATE GUIDE TO BILLIE EILISH

ONE BY ONE TOUR, DENMARK
Are you even a pop star until you've fallen over on stage? Billie was singing **'Bury a Friend'** when she slipped over on the floor. She lay on the floor for a few minutes and carried on singing from there. **What a pro.**

RADIO 1 LIVE LOUNGE
Billie did a cover of Phantogram's **'You Don't Get Me High Any More'** while wearing a skeleton hoodie. *"I might bomb it"* she said before she started, but of course she nailed it.

THE GREEK THEATRE, LA
For a stripped-back acoustic performance of **'I Love You'**, Billie and her brother Finneas performed on a floating bed, because they wrote the song on her bed at two in the morning. Billie dedicated the song to a friend who passed away and it was so poignant, many people there were reduced to tears, including Billie.

BAD GUY ON SNL
So what if she's got a sprained ankle, for this Halloween performance Billie Eilish literally climbed up the walls and danced on the ceiling. **Cooool.**

She often arrives on stage to music from a Nintendo Wii

100% UNOFFICIAL

BEST MUSIC VIDEOS

From the creepy to the, er, creepier, these are our favourite Billie videos

7 Bury a Friend

Like a mini horror movie, this video has Billie play a black-eyed monster hiding under the bed. She's then injected with needles, levitates in hallways, gets grabbed by disembodied hands and then watches someone sleep. Shivers.

6 You Should See Me In A Crown

Billie teamed up with artist and animator Takashi Murakami for this video, which features a cartoon Billie. It's cute until Billie transforms into a monster-size spider with a human skull face who destroys a city.

5 Idontwannabeyouanymore

Sometimes it's the simple things that can be the most effective, like this video! It is just Billie dressed in a white boiler suit, in a white room, looking at herself in the mirror. Weirdly it's captivating.

30

ULTIMATE GUIDE TO BILLIE EILISH

4 When the Party's Over
The shots of Billie crying thick black ink in this video were inspired by a drawing she received from a fan. Eilish actually had tubes on her face that spurted out the charcoal and gum solution into her eyes.

3 Xanny
Billie made her directorial debut with the video for this song. She looks normcore, with a brunette wig on a cream bench. And then hands enter and put cigarettes out on her face. Ouch!

2 Everything I Wanted
Also directed by Billie, this video is dedicated to Finneas and shows Billie and her brother going for a drive through LA. Then they drive into the ocean. The car fills with water and everything goes black.

1 bad guy
Bloody nose? Two heads in plastic bags? Pouring milk in someone's mouth? Sitting on someone's back while they do push-ups? No, it's not a fever dream, it's the video for bad guy of course!

100% UNOFFICIAL

BILLIE VS FAME

Think being a mega-famous pop star is all it's cracked up to be? Think again

It's a love / hate thing

Considering she virtually found fame overnight, it's not surprising Billie Eilish feels a bit ambivalent about it. "I hate it. But it's great, though. I don't mean that to sound ungrateful. It's a really hard thing and hurts, but who cares?" Mixed feelings then, we guess.

OK, sometimes it's just a hate thing

Billie doesn't want to dislike fame, but she's good at admitting that some parts are a drag. "I have this amazing thing in front of me, and I don't want to hate it. And I don't hate it. But I hate certain parts of it."

Household name

She now has the kind of notoriety where people stop her on the street. "It's like nothing I would ever think it is," she says. "When this kind of thing happens, you just have to be like, 'let's just go with it.'"

ULTIMATE GUIDE TO BILLIE EILISH

The good old days

But it wasn't always like this. "For a minute, I could go somewhere nobody knew who I was," she says. "I would go places and try to convince myself I wasn't famous or whatever."

It's lonely at the top

If you're one of Billie's mates, it can be hard to understand her fame. "I've definitely lost a lot of people. When I hang out with people I haven't seen in a while, I say the things that are going on in my life and people think I'm bragging. I'm not bragging, I'm just telling you about my life."

She won't let it go to her head

So don't expect her to start acting like a diva. "What I know is that I never want to feel famous in my head. I've already seen how gross it can make you."

But she likes it really …

"I like being famous. It's very weird, but it's very cool."

100% UNOFFICIAL

WHO IS FINNEAS?

He's waaaay more than just Billie's brother that's for sure

If you're a Billie fan you'll already know all about her big bro Finneas, who co-writes and produces all her songs. So what else do we know about him?

Finneas O'Connell was born on 20 July 1997 which makes him 5 years older than Billie.

If you recognise him, it might be because he played Alistair in the TV show Glee and also appeared in Modern Family.

Finneas is the lead singer THE SLIGHTLYS. That's actually who he wrote the song '*Ocean Eyes*' for originally.

34

ULTIMATE GUIDE TO BILLIE EILISH

He's been dating YouTuber Claudia Sulewski since 2018, and even wrote a song called '*Claudia*' about her which he wrote after the first night they met. *Aww.*

Along with writing songs for Billie, he's also written songs for YouTube singer Rebecca Black.

"We're a pretty close knit family to begin with so that's not really super new," says Finneas about touring with Billie. "We get along really well so it's been really nice."

"Me and Finneas have always had a bond," Billie revealed. "We've always had a connection, especially with music."

35

100% UNOFFICIAL

BILLIE'S FAVOURITE THINGS

We're all a fan of Billie, but what is she a fan of?

THE OFFICE

Billie is a big fan of the **Steve Carrell** show. So much so that she even sampled a song from the episode called **'Threat Level Midnight'**. *"When we made the beat for* **'My Strange Addiction,'** *it reminded me of the song they play when they do the Scarn dance. Also, it's about strange addictions, and* **The Office** *is mine, so …"*

JUSTIN BIEBER

Billie has made no secret about being a Belieber. *"It wasn't like I was just a fan, man. I've been in love before, and it was with him,"* she told Marie Claire. She finally got to meet him at Coachella, and the pair collaborated on a remix of **'bad guy'** so now they're totally mates.

AVOCADOS

And it's not just because she has green hair. Her Instagram handle used to be **WhereAreTheAvocados**. And here is why. *"Six years ago, I wanna say, I was in my house, home alone, making a grilled cheese,"* Billie said. *"I was almost done, you know, I was getting everything ready and I wanted some avocados, so I opened the fridge and was like, 'Where are the avocados?' And in my head I was like, that'd be funny if I made that my username."* So now we know.

ANIMALS

A vegan since 2014 and a keen horse-rider, Billie is a friend to furry creatures. *"Horses are the most therapeutic animals. And cows, dude. People eat those – that's crazy."* We'll never look at a burger in the same way again.

THE MOSH PIT

You know that scary part at the front of a gig where everyone is diving around going crazy? Billie loves it. *"I love movement. I love moshing. I always head right for the front and dig in there and mosh really hard with all the guys."*

100% UNOFFICIAL

THE ULTIMATE BILLIE PLAYLIST

There's a Billie tune for every mood

You're feeling whimsical …?
Play … Party Favor

This sweet-sounding tune from her debut EP 'Don't Smile At Me' is a twinkly, plinky soundscape about breaking up with someone on their birthday. This is as cute and catchy as Billie gets.

You're feeling shy …?
Play … Come Out and Play

Billie and Finneas wrote this song for the Apple Christmas advert and it's all about not hiding away and making your mark on the world. 'You don't have to keep it quiet / I know it makes you nervous / but I promise you it's worth it'.

ULTIMATE GUIDE TO BILLIE EILISH

**You're feeling fired up …?
Play … &burn**
In this collaboration with rapper Vince Staples, Billie delivers a bolshy, attitude-laden tune about watching someone's car burn, and her heart burn. Basically this song is on fire!

**You're feeling sassy …?
Play … Copycat**
'Call me cocky, watch your tone/You better love me, 'cause you're just a clone,' Billie commands on the opening track of her debut EP, 'Don't Smile At Me'. This song makes fans go crazy when Billie performs it live. "Psyche!"

**You're feeling loved-up …?
Play … Ocean Eyes**
From its opening whispers to its crooning chorus, Billie's breakthrough record is all about watching someone from afar, falling into their eyes and compares falling in love to falling off a cliff under "napalm skies".

**You're feeling creepy …?
Play … Bellyache**
Despite starting off as a twee slice of folk-pop, this gets dark. Billie adopts the mindset of a teenage serial killer slaughtering her nearest and dearest. Don't try this at home.

100% UNOFFICIAL

BILLIE OPENS UP

She's not afraid to tackle the big issues and say what's on her mind

DARK TIMES

Billie has been open about her battles with her mental health, helping millions of fans who also feel this way. *"Depression has controlled sort of everything in my life … I've kind of always been a melancholy person,"* she admitted to **Zane Lowe** on **Beats 1**. But she's used her struggles with her mood to help her fans. *"I just grab my fans by the shoulders and I'm like, "Please take care of yourself and be good to yourself and be nice to yourself."*

CLIMATE CHANGE

We're all worried about global warming, and Billie has been very vocal about her fears that we're not doing enough to stop it. *"It's weird …It feels like we're living in a movie that you'd watch where the world is like ending. I want to have children and I want them to have children."* At the **American Music Awards**, Billie wore a T-shirt showing her support for **'Music Declares Emergency'**, an activist group of artists and music professionals. Their mission to acknowledge the environmental impact of the music industry struck a chord with Billie, who has partnered with a non-profit company to keep her tour as green as possible.

BODY ISSUES

Wearing baggy clothes has now become Billie's signature style. But she recently revealed that the reason it came about was because puberty made her uncomfortable about her body. *"I just hated my body,"* she says. *"I would have done anything to be in a different one."* Thankfully Billie always wears what she wants to wear despite the criticisms, and is very vocal about women in the industry not being judged by these superficial standards.

ULTIMATE GUIDE TO BILLIE

UNOFFICIAL

ULTIMATE GUIDE TO BILLIE

VOICE OF A GENERATION

There's never been a pop star like Billie before, here's how she enscapsulates the zeitgeist ...

SHE'S HONEST
Billie is incredibly candid about what's really on her mind. She's open about the downsides of fame and isn't afraid to be vulnerable about her mental health issues and her Tourette's.

SHE OPTS OUT OF WEARING REVEALING CLOTHES
Billie's style rejects traditional ways of dressing according to gender, for example girls wearing super-tight clothes. Her stylist, **Samantha Burkhart**, said Eilish *"is not buying into the hypersexualised idea of what femininity is."*

SHE'S POLITICAL
Her songs deal with the issues that **Generation Z** are worried about. In **'All The Good Girls Go To Hell'**, she sings 'Hills burn in California/ My turn to ignore ya', which is about climate change. She also has strong opinions about the US president's views on climate change.

43

UNOFFICIAL

SCREEN IDOL

Billie's music on the big screen

'13 REASONS WHY' WE LOVE BILLIE

Billie has had two songs appear on the soundtracks to the **Netflix** series **'13 Reasons Why'**. **'Bored'** appeared during series one, and **'Lovely'** was on series two, right when Clay talks with Hannah for the last time before the funeral and finishes his semicolon tattoo.

ROMA

Billie also released a typically moody ballad – **'When I Was Older'** - for an album of songs inspired by **Alfonso Cuarón's** 2018 movie **'Roma'**. The song is inspired by something said by Pepe, a character in Roma, *"When I was older I used to be a sailor, but I drowned in a storm."* Billie and Finneas fell so in love with the film, which also won Best Foreign Language film at the **Oscars** and the **Golden Globes**, that they got to work on a new track.

THE NAME'S EILISH, BILLIE EILISH

In January 2020, it was confirmed that Billie was following in the footsteps of Adele and Sam Smith by recording the theme music to the **James Bond** movie **'Time to Die'**.

• • • • • • • • • • • • • • • • • • • •

Billie and Finneas have always been big fans of the franchise and writing the theme song is a dream come true. *"James Bond is the coolest film franchise ever to exist. I'm still in shock,"* Billie said.

ULTIMATE GUIDE TO BILLIE EILISH

NATURE
Like being in green spaces? So does Billie. She loves to take her ukelele up to the treehouse built by her dad. So cool.

THE NEIGHBOURHOOD
Watching this band in LA was Billie's first gig and she says '**Wiped Out**' by **The Neighbourhood** is the soundtrack to her life. "It touches on a lot of different emotions at once – I think that is a good description of how my year has been. Surreal and kind of really cool, but a lot of bad things also happened, so it is kind of a mix of everything."

HER MUM
Billie's mum Maggie goes everywhere with her and was one of her earliest role models. "She's been with me through all of this and [has been] taking me at my horrible self. She taught me how to write music … I could go on about her." Aww.

47

100% UNOFFICIAL

BILLIE EXPLAINS IT ALL

What's really going on in Billie's lyrics?

"She's a serial killer!"

"She's a monster!"

"She's trying to seduce your dad!"

Billie is certainly no 'one trick pony' when it comes to songwriting. She composes songs about anything and everything, which is why people of all ages and from all walks of life relate so strongly to her. Let's look at a few of her songs and what they're all about:

BAD GUY

Billie's iconic song makes fun of everyone who pretends to be something they are not. We all now know that if we call ourselves bad guys or rule breakers, we're probably not ...

BURY A FRIEND

In this song Billie remind us of the importance of thinking about and doing things for yourself rather than giving all of yourself, including your love, to someone, or something, else and losing yourself in the process.

IDONTWANNABEYOUANYMORE

This song is about the way Billie feels about herself and her battles with depression. She wishes she had more confidence and was more secure in her abilities. She gets really honest about how, at times in her life, she has felt sad every day, and how she sometimes doesn't want to be herself.

BELLYACHE

In this one Billie sings about a fictional psychopath who kills off their friends. They regret being a psychopath but don't really care. Ummm not sure we can relate to this one.

100% UNOFFICIAL

TIMES BILLIE EILISH WAS ALL OF US

She might be a superstar, but so many things about Billie have us shouting 'Same!'

SHE LOVES FREE STUFF

We all love free stuff and Billie now gets sent everything from jewellery to fake nails, but she's most excited about Nikes: 'All I wanted was a pair of Nikes, and I couldn't afford them. And now I have hundreds in my house. Unreal."

SHE'S STRUGGLED TO FIT IN

We've all had our moments of trying to fit in and be just like everyone else. And whilst Billie is very much her own person these days, even she also went through an uncertain phase when she was younger: "I tried to fit in ... It was the worst year ever."

ULTIMATE GUIDE TO BILLIE EILISH

SHE'S RELATABLE

Take this tweet for example. *"i just smiled at a manikin thinking it was a person"*. We've all been there.

SHE GETS DOWN

Billie has been very open about her mental health issues, but also what she does to manage them. *"It doesn't make you weak to ask for help. And you should be able to ask anyone for help, everyone has to help someone if they need it."*

SHE STILL LIVES AT HOME

In a two-bedroom bungalow with her mum, dad, a rescue cat, **Misha**, a rescue dog, **Pepper,** and her spider. *"I'm lucky to have a family that I like, and that likes me,"* she says. And she still has to clean her own room.

100% UNOFFICIAL

BILLIE VS SOCIAL MEDIA

It's not all 'likes', y'know

YOUTUBE
Billie has called out YouTubers who've dressed up like her to make prank videos. She asked people to *"please stop. It is not safe for you and it is mean to the people who don't know any better ... you make me look bad"*.

TWITTER
She has 3.5million followers on Twitter, but after going through a dark time when she was in Europe, she no longer handles her own Twitter account. Good on Billie for distancing herself from all the opinions.

INSTAGRAM
She is on Insta and her username used to be the enigmatic **@Wherearetheavocados**. She's now **@Billieeilish**. The first picture she ever posted was of her thumb. She says her favourite Instagram accounts are stylists and fashion designers such as **@bloodyosiris**, **@imran_potato**, and **trainer addict @liljupiter**.

ULTIMATE GUIDE TO BILLIE EILISH

BE POSITIVE

Billie often uses social media to ask her fans to play nice with each other, although she says she doesn't care if they're mean to her as she's so used it and it doesn't affect her as she has so much love and support.

USE WITH CAUTION

Billie understands the dangers of social media and warns her followers about it too. She knows that comments and images shared through social media can ruin friendships and your self-esteem too, so sees it as really dangerous. Take care out there everyone.

100% UNOFFICIAL

FAMOUS FANS

Billie's most A-list superfans, ranked

1
ELTON JOHN
Legendary star, song-writer and musician, Elton John, loves Billie and thinks she's a unique new talent. He can't wait to see her live. You know you've made it when Elton John's at your show!

2
LANA DEL REY
Billie and Lana Del Rey have a special musical connection as Billie cited Lana as one of her biggest influences. And the singer songwriter loves Billie right back! Us too, Lana. Us, too.

3
DAVE GROHL
The **Foo Fighters** frontman has said that his daughters are obsessed with Billie and he's likened the connection she has with her audience to the fans Nirvana had in the 1990s.

4
KATY PERRY
There were **Fireworks** when Katy met Billie at the legendary **Coachella Festival**. Katy even posted on Instagram celebrating Billie as a unique and rare new talent in the industry!

ULTIMATE GUIDE TO BILLIE EILISH

5 SHAWN MENDES
The "**Señorita**" singer gave Billie a big up on Twitter, telling his fans how talented she is. Billie also revealed in an interview that Shawn had texted her but she hadn't replied. Whoops!

6 NIALL HORAN
Billie has fans all over the world and pop royalty is no exception, which was clear when 1D's Niall Horan tweeted out that he was bopping along to Billie's awesome album.

7 DEMI LOVATO
Girl power! Pop princess Demi Lovato is a massive Billie fan, taking the time to listen to Billie's awesome music and sharing her love and admiration with her fans on Instagram.

8 THOM YORKE
Iconically weird and wonderful Radiohead front man, Thom Yorke, is a big fan of the way Billie follows her own path and does her own thing. She's her own person, just like Thom!

100% UNOFFICIAL

BILLIE ON LOVE

Although she's very private about her love life, this is what we know about Billie's heart

SHE'S A FAN OF SELF LOVE

"I'm in love with myself. ... I'm in love with her," she said, gesturing to herself. Something we should all be emulating!

HER FIRST KISS WAS A DISAPPOINTMENT

Eilish dished about her unfortunate experience at a concert in March 2018. *"Two years ago, I went to the movies with a boy,"* she recalled. *"Right after we kissed, he says, 'Wow, that was really not as magical at all as I thought it was going to be,'"* she shared. Ouch.

SHE DOESN'T WANT HER FANS TO LOVE HER

After her own experience with being a superfan of Justin Bieber, Billie is suprised at how her fans feel the same way about her. *"I do not mean to be putting anybody in the position I was in. That hurts."*

HER FIRST LOVE WAS JUSTIN BIEBER

"I can't even explain it to sound normal – I was in love with him. It was so miserable. It's not a good feeling to be in love with someone who doesn't know you exist." We get it - Justin Bieber = swoon!

57

100% UNOFFICIAL

THINGS BILLIE HATES

Haters gonna hate, but here are all the things which Billie dislikes

ULTIMATE GUIDE TO BILLIE EILISH

SMILING
Don't expect to see many pictures of Billie flashing a cheesy grin. She hates smiling and can often be seen with what she describes as *"resting brat face"*. We will totally channel this when someone tells us to cheer up.

GETTING OLD
Billie doesn't ever want to be old as, er, 27! We're not sure there's much you can do about that one.

FANS COMING TO HER HOUSE
When the singer's address was leaked online, overly-enthusiastic fans began showing up at Billie's childhood home, which understandably left her shaken.

NIGHTMARES
Her album might be called **'When We All Fall Asleep, Where Do We Go?'** but Billie doesn't go somewhere dreamy when she tucks in at night. She regularly experiences **night terrors** and **nightmares**.

DRUGS
Billie has never done any drugs and is quite outspoken about it. She wrote the song **'Xanny'** about her experiences of watching her friends drink at a party. Great attitude, Billie!

100% UNOFFICIAL

ALBUM NUMBER 2

Here's everything we know so far about Billie's second album

WILL THERE BE ANY COLLABORATIONS ON THE SECOND ALBUM?

Yes! Back in March, Spanish singer **Rosalia** tweeted a photo of her and Billie, captioning it with *"Can't wait to finish our song"*. The singer was mightily impressed with Billie's work ethic and passion, and by all accounts these two had great time in the studio together. We're not jealous at all … **Tyler the Creator** has also said he wants to team up. Billie is a big fan of the rapper and we think this collaboration would be a-maz-ing!

ULTIMATE GUIDE TO BILLIE EILISH

WHEN IS IT COMING OUT?

Although rumours swirled during summer 2019 that she was about to drop another album, Billie was quick to shoot them down. So don't hold your breath for a 2020 release. But don't worry, she's assured fans it's coming.

HOW FAR THROUGH MAKING IT IS SHE?

Finneas explains to fans that they're deep in the creative process working on the new material. He also indicated that they're making music while touring, which is easier without all the usual distractions at home.

100% UNOFFICIAL

SHE'S WATCHING US
Before each show, Billie is driven around adjacent to the venue to look through the windows at the fans waiting outside. Aww!

SHE THINKS WE LOOK SICK
Billie appreciates our style. Before her shows, Billie likes to check out what her fans are wearing. *"They always look really cool."* Cheers, Billie!

SHE'S HERE FOR US
Billie knows what it's like to be a superfan and wants to be the kind of artist who is approachable. *"I consciously have been the artist I would have wanted to have been a fan of growing up,"* she says.

ULTIMATE GUIDE TO BILLIE EILISH

BILLIE ♥ HER FANS

It's a mutual appreciation society

SHE LOVES FAN GIFTS
If you're thinking of making Billie something, join the queue. Billie is used to receiving gifts from fans. She has even received a stuffed blohsh – the human outline Billie uses as a symbol. Cute!

SHE SEES US AS HER FRIENDS
We're all in this together guys. Billie knows she can't be friends with everyone but if ever an opportunity arises, she loves hanging out with her fans. *"There's this group of girls I've met a couple times and they're cool as hell. I just was friends with them."* Can we be your friend, Billie?

CREDITS

Front cover: PICTURES: Jason Richardson / Alamy Images, Ivan Kamzyst / Alamy Images.
4-5: PICTURES: UPI / Alamy Images.
6-7: WORDS: The New York Times. PICTURES: Jason Richardson / Alamy Images, UPI / Alamy Images.
8-9: WORDS: NME, Ssense, Paper magazine, Coup de Main. PICTURES: Gonzales Photo / Alamy Images, ZUMA Press, Inc. / Alamy Images, Andie Mills / Alamy Images.
10-11: WORDS: Billboard, NME, Ssense. PICTURES: Kathy deWitt / Alamy Images, MediaPunch Inc /Alamy Images, WENN Rights Ltd / Alamy Images.
12-13: WORDS: Stereogum.com, Ssense. PICTURES: ZUMA Press, Inc. / Alamy Images.
14-15: PICTURES: Roberto Finizio / Alamy Images, Gonzales Photo / Alamy Images.
16-17: WORDS: Luxury Insider, NME. PICTURES: Gonzales Photo / Alamy Images, WENN Rights Ltd / Alamy Images, Paul Smith / Alamy Images, Jeffrey Mayer / Alamy Images.
18-19: WORDS: FemaleMag, Bustle, Yahoo. PICTURES: WENN Rights Ltd / Alamy Images, ZUMA Press, Inc. / Alamy Images, Image Press Agency / Alamy Images.
20-21: WORDS: Rolling Stone. PICTURES: dpa picture alliance / Alamy Images, WENN Rights Ltd / Alamy Images, Roberto Finizio / Alamy Images.
22-23: WORDS: Buzzfeed. PICTURES: MediaPunch Inc / Alamy Images, Image Press Agency / Alamy Images, Pacific Press Agency / Alamy Images, YouTube / Darkroom/Interscope Records.
24-25: WORDS: MTV News. PICTURES: Image Press Agency / Alamy Images, Darkroom/Interscope Records.
26-27: WORDS: LA Times, Seventeen. PICTURES: Zoonar GmbH / Alamy Images, ZUMA Press, Inc. / Alamy Images.
28-29: PICTURES: Andy Gallagher /Alamy Images, ZUMA Press, Inc. / Alamy Images, MediaPunch Inc / Alamy Images.
30-31: WORDS: Billboard, Soompi.com, New York Times, Metro. PICTURES: YouTube / Darkroom/Interscope Records.
32-33: WORDS: Tidal, Rolling Stone, New York Times, The Times. PICTURES: Image Press Agency / Alamy Images, Pacific Press Agency / Alamy Images.
34-35: WORDS: PopBuzz, Coup de Main. PICTURES: UPI / Alamy Images, Pacific Press Agency / Alamy Images.
36-37: WORDS: MTV News, Marie Claire, Elle, BBC. PICTURES: Pacific Press Agency / Alamy Images.
38-39: PICTURES: dpa picture alliance / Alamy Images, ZUMA Press, Inc. / Alamy Images, Darkroom/Interscope Records.
40-41: WORDS: US Vogue, NME, Beats1, PopBuzz, NPR. PICTURES: Pacific Press Agency / Alamy Images.
42-43: WORDS: Elle, Vogue Australia. Pictures: Andie Mills / Alamy Images.
44-45: WORDS: Variance Magazine. Pictures: MediaPunch Inc / Alamy Images.
46-47: WORDS: Elle, PopSugar. Pictures: dpa picture alliance / Alamy Images, WENN Rights Ltd / Alamy Images, PictureLux / The Hollywood Archive / Alamy Images, Pacific Press Agency / Alamy Images, Andie Mills / Alamy Images.
48-49: WORDS: NME, Vice, Altpress. PICTURES: ZUMA Press, Inc. / Alamy Images.
50-51: WORDS: The Times, Ad Council. PICTURES: Guy Bell / Alamy Images, ZUMA Press, Inc. / Alamy Images, UPI / Alamy Images.
52-53: WORDS: Elle, Harper's Bazaar, Billboard. PICTURES: dpa picture alliance / Alamy Images, Newscom / Alamy Images.
54-55: WORDS: Pigeons and Planes, The New York Times, Variety. PICTURES: ZUMA Press, Inc. / Alamy Images, Everett Collection Inc / Alamy Images.
56-57: WORDS: NME, 3voor12, The Guardian, Rolling Stone. PICTURES: Image Press Agency / Alamy Images, dpa picture alliance / Alamy Images, Ivan Kamzyst / Alamy Images.
58-59: WORDS: Harper's Bazaar, Rolling Stone, The Guardian, Paper magazine. PICTURES: Guy Bell / Alamy Images, dpa picture alliance / Alamy Images, MediaPunch Inc / Alamy Images, YouTube / Darkroom/Interscope Records.
60-61: WORDS: iHeart Radio, Apple Music. PICTURES: Gonzales Photo / Alamy Images, ZUMA Press, Inc. / Alamy Images.
62-63: WORDS: The Guardian, Tidal, Variety, Rolling Stone, Vanity Fair. PICTURES: Gonzales Photo / Alamy Images, MediaPunch Inc / Alamy Images, Per Grunditz / Alamy Images.
Back cover: PICTURES: Pacific Press Agency / Alamy Images.